The Lion Book of
Children's Prayers

About this book

Prayer is a natural human response to life and that is specially true of children. Often they will want to pray in their own words, but I believe that they will also enjoy using prayers chosen with them in mind. All fit the needs and experiences of the readers, through not all are in simple, modern speech. Some of the great Christian prayers of other ages have been included, which are still apt and full of meaning. The mix of ancient and modern, simple and more difficult illustrates the variety and scope of prayer.

    Each double page covers some aspect of living and includes prayers of many kinds. The pictures help the imagination of readers of all ages. The whole book is planned to give enjoyment and a happy experience of prayer whether at school, in church or at home in the family.

Mary Batchelor

The Lion Book of
CHILDREN'S PRAYERS

A LION BOOK

Published by
Lion Publishing plc
Sandy Lane West, Oxford, England
ISBN 0 7459 2794 7
Albatross Books Pty Ltd
PO Box 320, Sutherland, NSW 2232, Australia
ISBN 0 7324 0801 6

First edition 1977
Reprinted 1978, 1979, 1980, 1981, 1982, 1983, 1984,
1986, 1987, 1988, 1990, 1993
This edition 1994

Prayers compiled by Mary Batchelor

Photographs supplied by Ebenezer Pictures, as follows:
Jeremy Browne page 15; Susanna Burton page 9, 18, 21,
23, 24, 28, 31, 33, 36, 39, 45, 49, 52, 55, 57, 58, 64, 65, 74,
79, 80, 87; David Keel page 29; David and Janet Townsend
page 69; Daniel E. Wray pages 11, 13, 42, 63, 73.
Cover: Daniel E. Wray: front (top left and right);
Susanna Burton: all remaining photographs.

Illustrations by Robert Mills

Printed and bound in Malaysia

Contents

In the Morning

God's mercies are new every morning.
From Lamentations 3

I can say it to my family, I can say it to my friends,
I can say it at school—so I'll say it to you—
Good morning, God, you're Great!

May my mouth praise the love of God this morning.
O God, may I do your will this day.
May my ears hear the words of God and obey them.
O God, may I do your will this day.
May my feet follow the footsteps of God this day.
O God, may I do your will this day.

Prayer from Japan

Dear Lord Jesus, we shall have this day only
once; before it is gone, help us to do all the good
we can, so that today is not a wasted day.

From a prayer by Stephen Grellet (1773–1855)

Father, we thank you for the night,
And for the pleasant morning light;
For rest and food and loving care,
And all that makes the day so fair.
Help us to do the things we should,
To be to others kind and good;
In all we do at work or play
To grow more loving every day.

Now another day is breaking,
Sleep was sweet and so is waking,
Dear Lord, I promised you last night
Never again to sulk or fight.
Such vows are easier to keep
When a child is sound asleep.
Today, O Lord, for your dear sake,
I'll try to keep them when awake.

Ogden Nash

Thank you, God, for the daytime when I can be
awake and busy. Thank you for all there is for me
to do today: new things to find out, friends and
games to play with. Thank you for the sun that
gives us warmth and light to see by.

Our Homes

Jesus went in to stay with them.

From Luke 24

God of all our cities,
Each alley, street, and square,
Pray look down on every house
And bless the people there.

Lord Jesus, we are glad that you lived in a happy home.
Thank you for our family and for those who love and care
for us. May we love and help them.

Please God, look after all those who stay behind at home
when others go out to school, or work or play. Bless the
ones who are too young or too old to go, and those who
look after them. Bless those who get things ready for us
when we get home, and help us to say thank you to them.
    We pray especially for those who stay at home because
they are ill.

May the love of God our Father
Be in all our homes today:
May the love of the Lord Jesus
Keep our hearts and minds always:
May his loving Holy Spirit
Guide and bless the ones I love,
Father, mother, brothers, sisters,
Keep them safely in his love.

Visit, we beseech thee, O Lord, our homes and drive far
from them all the snares of the enemy: let thy holy angels
dwell therein to preserve us in peace; and may thy blessing
be upon us evermore; through Jesus Christ our Lord.

Your Beautiful World

And God saw everything that he had made,
and it was very good.

From Genesis 1

God, this is your world,
you made us, you love us;
teach us how to live in the world that you have made.

Loving Father,
we praise you for the wonderful things
which you have given to us:
For the beautiful sun,
For the rain which makes things grow,
For the woods and the fields,
For the sea and the sky,
For the flowers and the birds
And for all your gifts to us.
Everything around us rejoices.
Make us also to rejoice and give us thankful hearts.

Heavenly Father, thank you for the beauty and wonder of your great creation.

It's your world, God.
From the top of my favourite tree
There are lots of things to see,
Children are playing on the grass,
Mums with clothes pegs in their mouths,
Babies crying,
Nappies drying,
Grandpas smoking, soaking up the sun,
Watching this year's carrots come.
It's your world, God;
I like it.

Forgive Us, God

Forgive us the wrongs that we have done,
as we forgive the wrongs that others have done us.

From the Lord's Prayer, Matthew 6

Our Father in heaven:
Please forgive me for the wrongs I have done:
For bad temper and angry words;
For being greedy and wanting the best for myself;
For making other people unhappy:
Forgive me, heavenly Father.

O God, you made us and you love us, thank you for
being so willing to forgive us. Make us quick to own up to
you whenever we do wrong so that we may quickly be
forgiven. Then our day will not be spoilt and we can be
happy all day long, through Jesus Christ our Lord.

Lord Jesus Christ, we confess to you now
the wrong things we have done,
the wrong things we have said,
the wrong in our hearts: please forgive us
and help us to live as you want us to.

Lord Jesus, we remember how you forgave the people
who hurt you. Help us to forgive those who hurt us.
May we never try to pay them back.

Forgive me, Lord, for thy dear Son
The ill that I this day have done.
That with the world, myself, and thee,
I, ere I sleep, at peace may be.

Bishop Thomas Ken (1637–1711)

Animals and Pets

Lord, you have made so many things!
How wisely you made them all!
The earth is filled with your creatures.

From Psalm 104

All things bright and beautiful,
All creatures great and small,
All things wise and wonderful
The Lord God made them all.

He gave us eyes to see them,
And lips that we might tell
How great is God Almighty,
Who has made all things well.

Mrs C. F. Alexander (1818–95)

Our Father, thank you for our pets—for friendly cats
and dogs and rabbits. Help us to take great care of them.

Thank you for the beasts so tall
Thank you for the creatures small.
Thank you for all things that live
Thank you, God, for all you give.

Dear Lord Jesus, our little dog has died. We cried
because she was so loving and good. She made
everyone happy. We are glad it's you who've got
her now. Please take care of her, but of course you
will. You love all animals. You made them all.
Thank you for letting us have her first and for all
the happy times we've had with her.

Father, we thank you for animals that help us, for
cows, sheep and horses; dogs that guard us and those
that guide the blind. We thank you too for all rare
animals and for those that make us laugh. May we take
good care of them all.

Dear Father, hear and bless
Thy beasts and singing birds;
And guard with tenderness
Small things that have no words.

Help Us to Please You, God

Happy are those who obey God with all their heart.

From Psalm 119

Lord, through this day,
In work and play,
Please bless each thing I do.
May I be honest, loving, kind,
Obedient unto you.

Help us to keep the promises we make to you,
O God.

Open my eyes that I may see,
Incline my heart that I may desire,
Order my steps that I may follow
The way of your commandments.

Lancelot Andrewes (1555–1626)

Dear Lord Jesus, help us to please you by doing
as our teachers and parents tell us even when
we want to go our own way.

Day by day, dear Lord, of thee
three things I pray:
to see thee more clearly,
love thee more dearly,
follow thee more nearly,
day by day.

Richard of Chichester (about 1197–1253)

19

For Sad Days

In times of trouble God will . . . keep me safe.
From Psalm 27

Lord Jesus, I pray for those
who will be unhappy today:
for parents who have no food
to cook for their children;
for those who cannot earn
enough money for their families;
for children who are sick
or frightened;
and for those who are alone
and without people to love them.

Dear Lord Jesus, you cried when your friend Lazarus
died, so you understand how we are feeling today.
Comfort us as we are sad and lonely without the one we
loved so much. Help us to be glad that our friend is
happy with you and free for ever from sadness and pain.
Teach us to trust and love you so that we too may live
with you for ever.

Lord Jesus, you know that we are sad today.
Help us to cheer up, because you love us always
and are close to us all the time.

The Lord is my shepherd;
I have everything I need.
He lets me rest in fields of green grass
and leads me to quiet pools of fresh water.
He gives me new strength.

He guides me in the right way,
as he has promised.
Even if that way goes through deepest darkness,
I will not be afraid, Lord,
because you are with me!
Your shepherd's rod and staff keep me safe.

From Psalm 23

All the Countries of the World

God loved the world so much that he gave his only Son,
so that everyone who believes in him may not die
but have eternal life.

From John 3

Space counts for nothing, Lord, with thee;
Thy love enfolds each family
Across the ocean, far away,
And here at home where now we pray,
And praise thee for thy care this day.

Please guide the leaders of many different countries
at the meetings where they try, by working together, to
make the world a better and a safer place. Help them
to want peace rather than power, and show them how
they can share the food in the world so that no one
need be hungry.

Dear Father of the world family,
please take care of all children everywhere.
Keep them safe from danger,
and help them grow up strong and good.

O Lord, help us who roam about. Help us who have been placed in Africa and have no dwelling-place of our own. Give us back our dwelling-place. O God, all power is yours in heaven and earth.

Prayer of an African chief

God our Father, Creator of the world,
please help us to love one another.
Make nations friendly with other nations;
make all of us love one another like a family.
Help us to do our part to bring peace in the world
and happiness to all people.

Prayer from Japan

God Cares

Look at the birds flying around: they do not plant seeds,
gather a harvest and put it in barns; your Father in heaven
takes care of them! Aren't you worth much more than birds?

From Matthew 6

God, who made the grass,
The flower, the fruit, the tree,
The day and night to pass,
Careth for me.

When I wake up in the morning,
thank you, God, for being there.
When I come to school each day,
thank you, God, for being there.
When I am playing with my friends,
thank you, God, for being there.
And when I go to bed at night,
thank you, God, for being there.

I bind unto myself today
The power of God to hold and lead,
His eye to watch, his might to stay,
His ear to hearken to my need
The wisdom of my God to teach,
His hand to guide, his shield to ward;
The word of God to give me speech,
His heavenly host to be my guard.

St Patrick (389–461)

Lord, how glad we are that we don't hold you
but that you hold us.

Prayer from Haiti

For Happy Days

Sing for joy to the Lord, all the world!
From Psalm 100

Praise God, from whom all blessings flow;
Praise him, all creatures here below;
Praise him above, ye heavenly host;
Praise Father, Son and Holy Ghost.

Bishop Thomas Ken (1637–1711)

My heart is overflowing with praise of my Lord,
my soul is full of joy in God my Saviour. The one who can do
all things has done great things for me—oh, holy is his name!

From the Magnificat (Luke 1)

Let us with a gladsome mind
Praise the Lord for he is kind;
For his mercies shall endure,
Ever faithful, ever sure.

All things living he doth feed,
His full hand supplies their need:
For his mercies shall endure,
Ever faithful, ever sure.

John Milton (1608–1674)

Thank you for each happy day,
For fun, for friends and work and play;
Thank you for your loving care,
Here at home and everywhere.

O Father of goodness,
We thank you each one
For happiness, healthiness,
Friendship and fun,
For good things we think of
And good things we do,
And all that is beautiful,
Loving and true.

Prayer from France

Dear Father of us all, we thank you for all the happiness of every day. We thank you for all the good things you give to us. Help us to make other people happy too.

Thank you, God, for this new day
In my school to work and play.
Please be with me all day long,
In every story, game and song.
May all the happy things we do
Make you, our Father, happy too.

O God, look on us and be always with us that we may live happily.

Prayer of the Amazulu people

Our Families

God gives families to the lonely.

From Psalm 68

God bless all those that I love;
God bless all those that love me:
God bless all those that love those that I love
And all those that love those that love me.

From an old New England sampler

We thank you, God, that everyone who loves you belongs
to your family. You are our Father, we are your children.
Thank you, God, for the worldwide family of your people.
Thank you for our brothers and sisters the whole world over.

God bless all the aunties,
Who are kind to girls and boys;
God bless all the uncles
Who remember birthday toys.

Thank you, Lord, for grannies and grandads.
Thank you for the stories they tell us and the things
they help us make. Thank you that they have time to
tie up our shoes and take us for walks.
Please bless them all.

Dear Father, please take special care of children whose
mother or father has left home. Keep them safe, and help
them to know that you love them and are always near to
comfort them.

O God, the Father of all families,
make our family like the family where Jesus grew up,
and our home like his home, where we all care for
each other and share our things with each other,
so that there is enough for everyone. Show us what
to do when we feel jealous, or want our own way,
or don't want to help.

When We Feel Frightened

When I am afraid, I put my trust in you.
From Psalm 56

Lord Jesus, I'm scared. Help me.
I needn't be afraid, because you are with me.
You are stronger than anything. You love me.
You will take care of me. Thank you.

All by myself with the door shut and the light out
I'm afraid. It gets so dark I can't see and the noises
seem so loud. The stories of witches and shootings
and news on TV get all mixed up and seem very real.
I'm scared so I need you, Lord.

Jesus, when I am afraid, help me to remember that
you are with me, nearer than my breathing, closer than
my beating heart. You understand my fears better than
I do, so let me trust in you and help me to support
others in their fears as you support me.

When I know how much you love me, Jesus,
and that you're always with me,
I can talk to you about being afraid.
You understand. You won't laugh at me.
Give me courage, make me brave,
not just tonight—but tomorrow as well.

The King of love my Shepherd is,
Whose goodness faileth never
I nothing lack if I am his
And he is mine for ever.
Henry Williams Baker (1821–77)

O God, who knowest us to be set in the midst of so many and great dangers, that by reason of the frailty of our nature we cannot always stand upright; grant to us such strength and protection, as may support us in all dangers, and carry us through all temptations; through Jesus Christ our Lord.

Book of Common Prayer

Please Teach Us, God

Teach me your ways, Lord,
make them known to me.
Teach me to live according to your truth.

From Psalm 25

O Lord, open my eyes,
to see what is beautiful;
My mind, to know what is true:
My heart, to love what is good:
for Jesus' sake.

Teach us, good Lord, to serve thee as thou deservest;
To give and not to count the cost;
To fight and not to heed the wounds;
To toil and not to seek for rest;
To labour and not to ask for any reward
Save that of knowing that we do thy will.

Ignatius Loyola (1491–1556)

When I pray I speak to God, when I listen God speaks to me.
I am now in his presence. He is very near to me.

Lord Jesus, take me this day and use me.
Take my lips and speak through them.
Take my mind and think through it.
Take my will and act through it,
and fill my heart with love for you.

O God, make us children of quietness
and heirs of peace.

First-century prayer by St Clement

God be in my head, and in my understanding:
God be in mine eyes, and in my looking:
God be in my mouth and in my speaking;
God be in my heart, and in my thinking;
God be at my end, and at my departing.

From a Book of Hours (1514)

O make my heart so still, so still,
When I am deep in prayer,
That I might hear the white mist-wreaths
Losing themselves in air!

Utsonomiya San—Prayer from Japan

Our Friends

A friend loves at all times.

From Proverbs 17

Jesus, friend of little children,
Be a friend to me;
Take my hand and ever keep me
Close to thee.

Lord Jesus, you want us all to live together as friends,
sharing our differences and giving our help. Please teach
us to be loving, patient with the people who are slower
than us, and friendly with those who are shy.

Thank you, God, for friends.
Thank you for fun and games and parties.
Thank you for my best friend.
Help me to be a good friend and keep my
promises. Help me to be friends even with those
I don't much like—because you love us all.

Jesus, when you were on earth you had friends who were especially close to you. You knew what it was like to enjoy their company; you also knew what it was like when they deserted you. Please keep my friends in your care. Help me to be a good friend.

We thank you, loving God, that when we come to say sorry, you are always ready to forgive. Please help us to be like you. When people say sorry to us may we forgive them straightaway, ready at once to be friends again.

Helping and Caring

Help carry one another's burdens.

From Galatians 6

Thank you, O God our helper, for all who help you to look after us. For mothers and fathers, and all who look after us in our homes. For teachers who help us at school, and for all who teach us what you are like.

Lord, make me an instrument of thy peace;
Where there is hatred, let me sow love;
Where there is injury, pardon;
Where there is discord, union;
Where there is doubt, faith;
Where there is despair, hope;
Where there is darkness, light;
Where there is sadness, joy.

St Francis of Assisi (1182–1226)

Lord Jesus, show us something to do for you:
something loving to say, something kind to do,
somebody to comfort, something lovely to make.
Help us to watch with your eyes for chances to
do your work because we love you.

Thank you, God, for all good people; for people who are strong and brave when others are afraid; for people who help others to be happy and good; for people who are cheerful when things go wrong. Thank you, God, for all good people.

Two little eyes to look to God;
Two little ears to hear his word;
Two little feet to walk in his ways;
Two little lips to sing his praise;
Two little hands to do his will
And one little heart to love him still.

Summer Holidays and Vacation

The whole earth is full of God's glory.

From Isaiah 6

Dear God, thank you for our holidays:
for the sunshine, the fresh air,
the lovely open spaces and the sea.
Thank you for this chance to see other places
and to meet different people.

Thank you, God, our heavenly Father, for holiday
joys beside the sea. For pebbles and rocks and
shells and sand; for the blue sea and for the fun
of playing in the water.

We thank you, God, that you will be with us
today as we go on our outing. Please give us a
happy time. Keep us safe and help us to discover
new and interesting things.

Praise to God for summer days,
For summer clothes and summer plays,
And for our summer holidays.

Lord Jesus, be with those who have no happy holidays,
who have never seen the sea or played in the fields.
If there is something we can do to make them happier
please show us, and if there is something we can share,
help us to do it gladly for your sake.

Thank you, God, for holidays
In the lovely summer days,
For our picnics, for our fun,
For our playing in the sun.
Make us good, with smiling faces,
So our homes are friendly places,
And the helpful things we do
Make all our parents happy too.

When We Are Ill

The Lord will help him when he is sick
and restore him to health.

From Psalm 41

Lord Jesus, I am ill.
Please make me well.
Help me to be brave,
and thankful to the people
looking after me.
Thank you for being here with me.

You're marvellous, God, loving everyone the way you do.
I don't like having to stay in bed but when I talk to you.
I know you love me and that's great.
Some children always have to stay in and never
get out to make friends.
Love them too, and help them.

Lord Jesus, who for our sakes became a man, and who showed your love of children by taking them up in your arms and blessing them: we ask you to bless those who are ill. Your love for them is greater than ours can ever be; therefore we trust them to your care and keeping.

Great Father in heaven, thank you for doctors and nurses everywhere. Thank you for giving them clever brains to know how to make us well, and gentle hands to bandage cuts and sores.

Tend thy sick ones, O Lord Christ,
rest thy weary ones.
Bless thy dying ones.
Soothe thy suffering ones.
Pity thine afflicted ones.
Shield thy joyous ones.
And all for thy love's sake.

St Augustine (354–430)

Coming and Going

The Lord will protect you as you come and go.
From Psalm 121

Thank you, God, for the fun of travelling. Thank you for planes and helicopters, ships and yachts, for rockets and spacecraft, underground trains and escalators; for cars and trains, motor-bikes and lorries. Please watch over all who travel today. Give them common sense and politeness. Teach them to guard against accidents and to obey the rules made for their safety.

Loving heavenly Father, who takes care of us all,
please bless all the people on the roads today:
please bless the people driving buses, cars and lorries,
please bless the people riding bicycles and scooters,
please bless the people walking and crossing busy roads,
please help them to be careful on the roads today
and help us to be careful when we cross the roads.

Alone with none but thee, my God,
I journey on my way.
What need I fear, when thou art near,
O King of night and day?
More safe am I within thy hand
Than if a host did round me stand.

St Columba (521–597)

God of all the steamships sailing far away,
God of all the railways running every day,
God of all the travellers on bus or car or plane,
Guard and guide them every one and bring them home again.

Bless all those I shall meet today, and help us to
help each other.

Hot Days and Cold Days

While the earth remains, cold and heat,
summer and winter shall not cease.
From Genesis 8

O ye summer and winter, bless ye the Lord,
Praise him and magnify him for ever.

Benedicite

Heavenly Father, thank you for the joys of winter:
for snow and wind, and sparkling frost;
for cosy fires and indoor games;
for warm clothes, and the shelter of our homes
on stormy nights; thank you, heavenly Father.

Dear God, who made the world, we thank you for the winter.
We thank you for the cold, frosty days, when we jump and
run and keep warm; for snow and the fun we have with it;
for warm clothes and good fires and hot dinners.

Wind and ice and shrouding snow
At thy bidding come and go;
Clouds obscure or planets shine,
But they serve thee and are thine.

We thank you for the beautiful
snow, for the warmth it gives to
the earth, and for its quietness.
Help us to be quiet enough
to hear your voice speaking to us
and to obey it always.

Dear Father God, who made the world, we thank you
for the summer. We thank you for the warm sunny days,
for our summer clothes, for the games we play out of doors
and all the nice things that summer brings.

We thank you, O loving Father,
for the joys that summer brings;
for warm days and soft breezes,
for the trees and the flowers.
Help us to remember
that all lovely things come from you.

Time for Play

For everything its season and for every activity its time.
From Ecclesiastes 3

Dear God, thank you for our toys—big ones and little ones, old and new ones, the ones we play with, the ones we take to bed with us. Help us to share our toys with other children and to say 'thank you' to the people who gave them to us.

Dear God, thank you for books: big serious ones, thin funny ones, books with pictures and books that tell stories; and thank you for the people who write them.

Give me, Lord, each day,
time to pray,
time to serve and love,
time to work and create,
time to do nothing
and time to be still.

Loving Father, on this day
Make us happy in our play,
Kind and helpful, playing fair,
Letting others have a share.

Dear God, we enjoy watching programmes on television,
especially those which are exciting and interesting.
Thank you for all the people who make the programmes—
the performers and producers,
the camera crew and engineers,
and those who write the stories and play the music.

Our Father, maker of this wonderful world,
thank you for Saturday, for holiday time
and freedom and the open air.
Come into all I am going to do today
at home, out of doors, with my friends.
Help me to enjoy everything
you have made for me.
For Jesus' sake.

Thank you, God, for music, for cheerful songs and sad tunes
too. Thank you for singers, bands and orchestras that play
for us. Thank you for the fun of making music for ourselves.

For the Light

God is light and in him is no darkness at all.
From 1 John

May the Lord Jesus Christ, who is the splendour of the
Eternal Light, chase far away all darkness from our hearts,
now and for evermore.

Praise him, sun and moon;
praise him all you shining stars!

From Psalm 148

O thou great Chief, light a candle within my heart that I
may see what is therein and sweep the rubbish from thy
dwelling place.

Prayer of an African girl

God, who hast folded back the mantle of the night
to clothe us in the golden glory of the day,
chase from our hearts all gloomy thoughts
and make us glad with the brightness of hope.

Ancient Collect

Thank you, God, for my eyes.
Thank you for the beauty of the world.
Thank you for all that my sight does for me.
Please support those who have no sight.
Please help me to remember the needs of the blind.
Please help me to remember that blind people
are ordinary people who cannot see.
Thank you, God, for my eyes.

Loving and Giving

We love because God first loved us.

From 1 John 4

Love and praise to you we give
By whose love all creatures live.

Father in heaven, we praise you that so many people love us.
Thank you most of all for your own great and wonderful love.
Make us loving too. Grant that we may show our love by
helping other people, for the sake of Jesus.

Put love into our hearts, Lord Jesus—love for you;
love for those around us; love for all we find it hard to like.

O Lord, help us to put you first; others next;
and ourselves last, now and always.

Help us, Lord, to be thankful for the gifts we
have received from you and to share with others
who are in need.

Lord of the loving heart, may mine be loving too,
Lord of the gentle hands, may mine be gentle too.
Lord of the willing feet, may mine be willing too,
So may I grow more like you
In all I say or do.

Eternal God, the light of the minds that know thee,
the joy of the hearts that love thee,
the strength of the wills that serve thee;
Grant us so to know thee that we may truly love thee,
so to love thee that we may fully serve thee,
whom to serve is perfect freedom.

Gelasian Sacramentary

Busy Days

Work, for I am with you, says the Lord.
From Haggai 2

Thank you for the joy that comes when we have done
a good piece of work, even if it means doing it over
and over again, as Jesus did in the carpenter's shop.
Thank you for the happy times we have when we do
things together, and share everything with each other.
Thank you for all our friends.

The things, good Lord, that we pray for,
give us grace to work for.

Sir Thomas More (1478–1535)

52

Dear Jesus, bless my hands today,
And may the things they do
Be kind and loving, strong and good,
Two busy hands for you.

Dear Lord Jesus, help us to enjoy the jobs we do to help
today: at home, when we clear away our toys or wipe the
dishes; at school, when we give out books and tidy our
classroom. May we do everything cheerfully and well,
because we love you.

Be my guide, O Lord, I pray,
Lest I stumble on my way.
Be my strength, dear Lord, I ask,
That I may fulfil each task.

Teach me, my God and King,
In all things thee to see,
And what I do in anything
To do it as for thee.

George Herbert (1539–1633)

Please Help

When Jesus saw this large crowd, his heart was filled with pity for them.
From Mark 6

Dear Father God, we thank you that we are able to see
—please help the blind.
We thank you that we are able to hear
—please help the deaf.
We thank you that we are able to speak
—please help the dumb.
We thank you that we can run and jump and play
—please help sick and disabled children everywhere.

O God, who made the world
And all the people in it,
We pray for boys and girls
Who've never heard of you:
We pray that they may come to know
You are the loving Father
Of every girl and boy.

Heavenly Father, bless those who starve while we have
plenty to eat; those who are homeless while we lie safely
in bed; those who have no clothes while we throw clothes
away. Help us to care for those less fortunate than
ourselves and to do all we can to help them.

Dear Jesus, you were taken as a baby refugee into Egypt, take care of all homeless wanderers, of all who have to leave their comfortable homes because of misfortune or war, and of all who have no homes at all. Guide them with your love to find help and friends, and to help each other in their loneliness.

Lord Jesus, we remember today the old people living around us. Especially we think of those who are lonely and poor and have no one to visit them or take them out. Please help us not to forget them. Help them to know that you are the Friend who never leaves us or forgets us.

We Praise You, God

O come, let us worship and bow down,
let us kneel before the Lord, our Maker!
From Psalm 95

Dear God, you are so very wonderful: more wonderful than the flowers, more wonderful than the sky, more wonderful than the sun. We praise you; we bless you; we worship you.

Holy God who madest me
And all things else to worship thee,
Keep me fit in mind and heart,
Body and soul, to take my part.
Fit to stand and fit to run,
Fit for sorrow, fit for fun,
Fit for work and fit for play,
Fit to face life day by day.
Holy God, who madest me,
Make me fit to worship thee.

Lord, thy glory fills the heaven,
Earth is with its fullness stored;
Unto thee be glory given,
Holy, holy, holy Lord.

Bishop R. Mant (1776–1848)

God, our loving Father, thank you that you never change. You are as strong and wise and loving as the day you made the world. Thank you that nothing can ever happen that will make you alter. You are the one true God and Maker of all. We worship you in Jesus' name.

For Our School

Whatever you do, work at it with all your heart.
From Colossians 3

O Lord, bless our school; that working together and playing together, we may learn to serve you and to serve one another.

Dear Jesus, I don't always like school. Some things are fun to learn; others are difficult. Was it the same when you had to learn things? Please help me to learn and to do my best at school.

Father of all, thank you for boys and girls of other lands who go to our schools. Give them courage as they live and work with those whose words and ways are so different from their own, and help us to be especially loving and friendly to them.

Father of us all, thank you for another happy day at school. Thank you for the new lessons we have learnt and the games we have played. May we come back tomorrow ready for another happy day.

O God, our heavenly Father, we are so very glad about the things we do in school: for the pictures we can paint, for the things we can make, for the books we can read, for the letters we can write, for the stories that we hear, for our music and our dancing, for the games that we can play, for our toys and for our friends. For all that we can do in school, for all our happy times in school, thank you, heavenly Father.

Thank you, God, for all our teachers
who come to school each day,
and for the teacher in our class
who helps us with our work.

Wet Days and Windy Days

God provides rain for the earth, he sends the wind.
From Psalm 147

Our Father in heaven, we praise you for the gift of rain;
thank you for giving rain to make the trees and flowers grow;
thank you for sending rain so that we may have water to
drink; thank you for the summer rain that cools the hot
dry earth.

Thank you, God, for rain and cool water,
which we need each day for washing and for bathing.
Help us not to grumble when a rainy day stops us
going out to play.

Thank you, heavenly Father,
for the wind that dries and warms the earth
so that seeds may grow, giving us food to eat
and flowers to see and smell.
Thank you too for fun outdoors on windy days.

Thank God for rain
and the beautiful rainbow colours
and thank God for letting children
splash in the puddles.

A child's own prayer

Dear Lord Jesus, who did not fear the sea,
guard all fishermen and sea-going people.
If danger comes, help them to be calm and courageous
and be with the people who answer their call for help.

Dear God, be good to me, the sea is so wide
and my boat is so small.

Prayer of the Breton Fishermen

Praised be our Lord for the wind and the rain,
For clouds, for dew and the air;
For the rainbow set in the sky above
Most precious and kind and fair.
For all these things tell the love of our Lord,
The love that is everywhere.

Elizabeth Goudge

Thank You, God

Give thanks to the Lord, for he is good.
From Psalm 106

Thank you, God, for this sunny morning,
it makes me happy.
A child's own prayer

Holy God, I'm happy that I can bow in prayer before you.
Thank you very much. Thank you for the clothes that we wear,
and everything you give us, and for forgiving us our sins.
As you died on the cross for us, be with us always.
Prayer of a Navajo Indian girl

For sausages, baked beans and crisps
For papers full of fish and chips
For ice cream full of chocolate bits
Thanks, God.

For furry caterpillars to keep
For woodlice with their tickly feet
For crabs we catch with bits of meat
Thanks, God.

For bicycles and roller skates
For playing football with my mates
For times when I can stay up late
Thanks, God.

Dear Father God, thank you for loving and caring for us
every day of our lives. Help us to remember your love,
and to love you in return.

Thank you for the world so sweet,
Thank you for the food we eat.
Thank you for the birds that sing,
Thank you, God, for everything.

People at Work

Do your work cheerfully, then, as though you served the Lord.
From Ephesians 6

Dear God, please look after everybody at work today: all those who drive buses and trains so that other people may go to work; those who work in mines and quarries to get material for others to use in factories and workshops; those who look after crops and animals on the farms to help with our food; those who catch fish for us to eat; those who bring our food to us and those who sell it in the shops. Bless all those who help to look after us.

O God, help us to remember the people working at night while we are asleep: for police officers walking in dark streets, and for the firefighters watching for sudden fires; thank you, God. For engine drivers rushing their great trains through the night; thank you, God. For the people working in busy factories; thank you, God.

Please bless those who have no work,
especially if they have had none for a long time.
They must be very bored and unhappy.
Please help their families to help them
and give them some work to do soon.

Dear God, we pray for the workers of the world.
For those who care for animals and those who grow our food.
For those who mine the coal, and those who run the trains.
For those who buy and sell, and those who keep the house.
For those who tend the sick, and those who keep us well.
For those whose work is dangerous, and those whose work
    is dull.
Dear God, we pray for the workers of the world.

Your Word, the Bible

Your word is a lamp to my feet
and a light to my path.
From Psalm 119

Father, we thank you for the Scriptures
which were written for our help and instruction.
Open our eyes to see the lessons that we can learn
from them.

Thank you, Lord, for those who gave their lives to give
us the Bible in our own language. Please help those who
are translating and printing the Bible in faraway places,
so that one day the Bible may be read in all the languages
of the world. Bless those who teach us to understand what
the Bible means, in our own country as well as in other lands.

O God, please comfort all the people who want to read
the Bible but live in countries where they are not allowed to.
Please help them to remember any verses they learned by
heart a long time ago.

Lord, here is my Bible,
here is this quiet room,
here is this quiet time,
and here am I.
Open my eyes;
open my mind;
open my heart; and speak.

Blessed Lord, who hast caused all holy Scriptures to be
written for our learning; grant that we may in such wise hear
them, read, mark, learn, and inwardly digest them, that by
patience and comfort of thy holy Word we may embrace and
ever hold fast the blessed hope of everlasting life, which thou
hast given us in our Saviour, Jesus Christ.

Book of Common Prayer

At Night Time

As soon as I lie down, I go quietly to sleep;
you alone, Lord, keep me perfectly safe.

From Psalm 4

Lord, keep us safe this night,
Secure from all our fears.
May angels guard us while we sleep,
Till morning light appears.

We thank you our heavenly Father, through Jesus Christ,
your dear Son, that you have graciously kept us this day;
and we pray that you would forgive us all our sins where
we have done wrong, and graciously keep us this night.
For into your hands we commend ourselves, our bodies
and souls, and all things. Let your holy angel be with us,
that the wicked Foe may have no power over us.

Martin Luther (1483–1546)

O God, my Guardian, stay always with me.
In the morning, in the evening,
by day, or by night, always be my helper.

Prayer from Poland

Good night! Good night!
Far flies the light;
But still God's love
Shall flame above,
Making all bright.
Good night! Good night!

Victor Hugo (1802–85)

Now the busy day is done,
Father, bless us every one.
Keep us safely through the night,
Till we see the morning light.

Heavenly Father, as people turn to sleep,
please bless all those who cannot sleep tonight.
Comfort those who are sad.
Forgive those who have done wrong.
Calm those who are worried.
Help those who are in pain.
And grant your peace to every troubled heart.

Jesus, tender Shepherd, hear me;
Bless your little lamb tonight;
Through the darkness please be near me;
Keep me safe till morning light.

All this day your hand has led me,
And I thank you for your care;
You have warmed and clothed and fed me
Listen to my evening prayer.

O Lord Jesus Christ, who received the children who came
to you, receive also from me, your child, this evening prayer.
Shelter me under the shadow of your wings, that in peace
I may lie down and sleep; and waken me in due time, that I
may glorify you, for you alone are righteous and merciful.

Prayer used in the Eastern church

Special Prayers
for Special Times

Christmas

Joyful news for everyone! The Saviour has been born.
From Luke 2

O Lord Jesus, who for love of us
lay as a baby in the manger, we
thank you that by your coming
you brought joy to all the world.
Help us at this glad time to try to
make others happy for your sake.

Thank you, God, for the joys of Christmas:
for the fun of opening Christmas stockings;
for Christmas trees with sparkling lights; for exciting parties;
for Christmas cakes and puddings; thank you, God.
Thank you for all the happiness of Christmas-time;
thank you for all the lovely presents we receive;
thank you most of all that Jesus was born as a baby
on the first Christmas Day.
Thank you, God.

Grant, heavenly Father, that as we keep
the birthday of Jesus, he may be born again
in our hearts, and that we may grow in the
likeness of the Son of God, who for our sake
was born Son of Man.

Jesus Christ, thou child so wise,
Bless mine hands and fill mine eyes,
And bring my soul to Paradise.
Hilaire Belloc

Dear baby Jesus, we have come to find you
in the stable at Bethlehem.
May we love you as Mary loved you.
May we serve you as Joseph served you.
May we worship you as the angels worshipped you,
Jesus, our King.

Easter

Jesus was given over to die because of our sins
and was raised to life to put us right with God.

From Romans 4

Good Friday is a time of sadness,
Easter is a time of gladness.
On Good Friday Jesus died,
But rose again at Eastertide.
All thanks and praise to God.

Jesus, you're alive!
Not as you were alive in Galilee with your friends.
Then only the people who met you could talk to you—
but now, everybody can.
   I'm talking to you and you're with me;
friends of yours all over the world are talking to you
now, this very minute, and you're with them.
   That's what I like about you—alive for everyone.

Jesus, who died for me,
Help me to live for thee.

Jesus, our Lord, we praise you that nothing
could keep you dead in the grave.
You are stronger than death and the devil.
Help us to remember
that there is nothing to be afraid of,
because you are alive and by our side.

Whitsun/Pentecost

God has sent the Spirit of his Son into our hearts.
From Galatians 4

Holy Spirit, hear us,
Friend from heaven above.
Thou art ever near us;
Fill our hearts with love.

We thank you, heavenly Father,
that when Jesus went back to be with you in heaven
you sent us the Holy Spirit to take his place.
Though we cannot see him, we know he is at work
in the world in everything that is good and holy,
and in our lives to carry out your will.
Send us the Holy Spirit, we pray, to shape and
mould our lives and guide us day by day.

O God, we cannot do your will unless you help us.
Send the Holy Spirit into our hearts to show us how to live.

Dear Holy Spirit, you are the one who comes along beside us to help and comfort us. Please make us sure that you are with us. You are the teacher who helps us to understand and remember what the Bible says. May we learn from you. You are God who comes to live in our hearts and love us. Help us to welcome you. For Jesus' sake.

O Lord our God, give us by thy Holy Spirit
a willing heart and a ready hand
to use all thy gifts to thy praise and glory;
through Jesus Christ our Lord.

Archbishop Cranmer (1489–1556)

O God, forasmuch as without thee we are not able to please thee; mercifully grant that thy Holy Spirit may in all things direct and rule our hearts; through Jesus Christ our Lord.

Book of Common Prayer

Harvest and Thanksgiving

Every good gift and every perfect gift is from above,
and comes down from the Father.

From James 1

O thou who art Lord of the harvest,
The Giver who gladdens our days,
Our hearts are for ever repeating
Thanksgiving and honour and praise.

Dear God our Father, we thank you for all your care for us;
for our homes and food and clothes; for our teachers and
our friends; and especially for our fathers and mothers.
Help us always to be thankful to you for all your great
goodness.

Blessed art thou, O Lord our God, King of the universe,
who bringest forth bread from the earth.

Jewish blessing

Bread is a lovely thing to eat—
God bless the barley and the wheat;
A lovely thing to breathe is air—
God bless the sunshine everywhere;
The earth's a lovely place to know—
God bless the folks that come and go!
Alive's a lovely thing to be—
Giver of life—we say—bless thee!

All good gifts around us
Are sent from heaven above;
Then thank the Lord,
O thank the Lord,
For all his love.

German hymn by Matthias Claudius (1740–1815)

Thank you, our heavenly Father, for harvest time:
for ripe fruit in the orchards and berries in the hedges:
for the vegetable harvest and all food gathered in
and stored for winter days.

Sunday

This is the day which the Lord has made;
let us rejoice and be glad in it.

From Psalm 118

O God and Father of us all, help us to feel the joy
of sharing in the worship and praise of people in other
countries. May the children who sing the same praises
as ours know that we join with them in praising and in
showing our love for you as they do.

For this new Sunday with its light,
For rest and shelter of the night,
We thank you, heavenly Father.
Through this new week but just begun,
Be near, and help us every one
To please you, heavenly Father.

Thank you, God, for our church and for the people there
who have taught me about you. Thank you, too, for the
people who worship and work for you in churches all round
the world. It's great to belong to this big worldwide family.

O Almighty God,
we thank you for this special day
which you have given us for worship and rest.
Help us to keep it holy,
as the best day in all the week.
Teach everyone to love and honour your day,
that we may all rejoice and be glad in it.

Seven whole days, not one in seven,
I will praise thee;
In my heart, though not in heaven,
I can raise thee.

George Herbert (1593–1632)

Birthdays

This is the word of the Lord, 'I have called you by name and you are my own.'

From Isaiah 43

O loving God, today is my birthday.
For your care from the day I was born until today
and for your love, I thank you.
Help me to be strong and healthy,
and to show love for others, as Jesus did.

Prayer from Japan

Thou who hast given so much to me
Give one thing more, a grateful heart.

George Herbert (1593–1632)

Lord, we thank you for this and every happy birthday;
as we grow in age and strength may we grow also in the
knowledge of your love and become more like you.

Lord Jesus, please help us to remember that you think it is
better to give things than to get them. Please teach us to be
givers, giving our time to help at home, giving turns to each
other at play, and giving our best work at school.

My Father, all last year you took care of me and now you
have given me a birthday. I thank you for all your goodness
and kindness to me. You have given me loving parents, a
home, gifts and clothes. Thank you, God. Help me to be a
better child in my new year, to grow strong, to study well,
to work happily.

Prayer from India

Graces

Jesus took the bread, gave thanks to God
and distributed it to the people.

From John 6

Each time we eat,
may we remember God's love.

Prayer from China

Bless, dear Lord, my daily food.
Make me strong and make me good.

Come, dear Lord Jesus, be our guest,
And bless what thou hast given us.

German grace

Thank you, Father, for this food,
Which you gave to do us good
Help us to remember you
All day long, in all we do.

We thank thee, Father, for thy care
For all thy children everywhere.
As thou dost feed us all our days
May all our lives be filled with praise.

Be present at our table, Lord;
Be here and everywhere adored.
Thy creatures bless, and grant that we
May feast in paradise with thee.

John Wesley (1703–91)

Bless me, O Lord, and let my food strengthen me to serve thee, for Jesus Christ's sake.

From The New England Primer

For every cup and plateful,
God make us truly grateful.

Some ha'e meat, and canna eat,
And some wad eat that want it;
But we ha'e meat, and we can eat,
And sae the Lord be thankit.

Robert Burns (1759–96)

Prayers for God's Blessing

Jesus took them in his arms and blessed them,
laying his hands upon them.

From Mark 10

God be merciful to us and bless us: and give us grace to
know his will and strength to do it.

The Lord bless us and keep us;
the Lord make his face shine upon us
and be gracious unto us:
the Lord lift up his countenance upon us,
and give us peace.

From Numbers 6

Be near me, Lord Jesus, I ask thee to stay
Close by me for ever, and love me, I pray.
Bless all the dear children in thy tender care;
And fit us for heaven to live with thee there.

J. T. MacFarland

God the Father, bless us;
God the Son, defend us;
God the Spirit, keep us
Now and evermore.

The grace of the Lord Jesus Christ
and the love of God
and the fellowship of the Holy Spirit
be with you all.

From 2 Corinthians 13

Prayers of Jesus

We ought always to pray and not lose heart.

From Luke 18

Our Father in heaven,
hallowed be your name,
your kingdom come;
your will be done,
on earth as in heaven.
Give us today our daily bread.
Forgive us our sins
as we forgive those who sin against us.
Lead us not into temptation
but deliver us from evil.
For the kingdom, the power, and the glory
are yours
now and for ever.

Father
May your name be kept holy,
May your Kingdom come.
Give us day by day the food we need.
Forgive us our sins,
For we forgive everyone who has done us wrong.
And do not bring us to hard testing.

From Luke 11

I thank you, Father, that you listen to me.
I know that you always listen to me.

From John 11

I pray for . . . those you gave me. Holy Father, keep them safe
by the power of your name—the name you gave me—so they
may be one just as you and I are one.

Jesus' prayer for his disciples, from John 17

Now my heart is troubled—and what shall I say?
Shall I say, 'Father, do not let this hour come upon me'?
But that is why I came, to go through this hour of suffering.
O Father, bring glory to your name!

From John 12

Forgive them, Father!
They don't know what they are doing.

Jesus' prayer from the cross, from Luke 23

Subject Index

This list supplements, and is designed to be used in conjunction with, the main contents list. Figures in bold type indicate a main theme as distinct from individual prayers.

Index of First Phrases

Acknowledgments

We would like to thank all those who have given us permission to include their prayers in this book, as indicated in the list below.

Every effort has been made to trace and contact copyright owners. If there are any inadvertent omissions or errors in the acknowledgments, we apologize to those concerned and will remedy these in the next edition.

Baker Book House: 25(d) from *God Is No Stranger* by Sandra L. Burdick

Mary K. Batchelor: 17(b), 19(b), 20(b), 20(c), 29(a), 29(b), 47(d), 66(b)

Blandford Press Ltd: 18(a), 22(c), 27(c), 27(d), 29(c), 37(a), 37(d), 38(d), 45(a), 47(a), 52(a), 61(a), 62(a), 62(d), 65(b), from *The Infant Teacher's Prayer Book* 50(d), from *The Junior Teacher's Prayer Book*, all edited by D.M. Prescott

Su Box: 58(b), 81(c)

Church Missionary Society: 39(a), 39(b), 44(b), 51(b), 72(a), from *All Our Days*, edited by Irene Taylor and Phyllis Garlick

Church Pastoral-Aid Society: 14(a), 67(a), by Dick Williams, 15(a) by Christopher Idle, from *Prayers for Today's Church*; 22(b) by Beryl Bye from *Please God*

Community of the Glorious Ascension: 75(b)

Concordia Publishing House: 86(d) from *Little Folded Hands*

Duckworth and Co. Ltd: 61(d), from *Thanksgiving for the Earth*

Elizabeth Fisher: 27(b)

Hodder and Stoughton Ltd: 30(c) 35(a), 46(c), 48(e), from *A Patchwork Prayer Book*, Janet Lynch-Watson; 72(b), 72(d), from *Prayers for the Home*, Brenda Holloway; 10(b), 15(b), 16(b), 17(a), 41(b), 50(b), 59(a), 60(a), from *Prayers for Younger Children* Brenda Holloway; 12(a), 64(b), from *Prayers for Children and Young People* compiled by Nancy Martin; 38(a), 46(a), 46(b), 47(b), 55(b), 70(b), 76(b), from *Well God, Here We Are Again*, John Bryant and David Winter

Mrs Beryl Kerr: 37(e) from the CSSM *Chorus Book*, published by Scripture Union

Ladybird Books Ltd: 38(b), 60(b), 60(c), 79(b), from the former *Ladybird Book of Prayers Through the Year* by H.I. Roston

Lutterworth Press: 44(d) from *Children's Prayers and Praises*, Ella Forsyth Wright; 53(c) from *A Book of Prayers for Boys and Girls*, Elfryda Wightman

Nancy Martin: 14(b), 61(b), 65(a), from *Prayers for Childen and Young People*, published by Hodder & Stoughton

Mowbray and Co. Ltd: 10(a) 43(c), from *God of All Things*; 43(d), 50(c), from *Talking to God*; 83(a) from *The Lord is my Shepherd*

Ogden Nash: 9(a), copyright © 1962 Ogden Nash. Reprinted by permission of Curtis Brown Ltd. In North America, from *Custard and Company* by Ogden Nash. Copyright © 1961, 1962 by Ogden Nash. By permission of Little, Brown and Company

National Christian Education Council: 22(a), 81(a) from *Missionary Prayers and Praises*, H.I. Rostron

The National Society for Promoting Religious Education: 32(c) from *Worship in Junior Schools*; 75(c) from *Thy Kingdom Come*; 32(d) by R.R. Broakes from *Unto the Hills*; 16(c), 81(d), by H.W. Dobson from *In Excelsis*; 8(a), 13(b), 30(b), 30(d), 40(b), 62(c), from *Prayabout* by Heather Howell; 63(a) from *Hymns and Songs for Children*

Oxford University Press: 10(d), 25(b), 43(a), 54(b), 56(a), 59(b), 59(c), 73(a), from *Infant Prayer*, Margaret Kitson; 10(c), 51(a), 55(a), 64(a), from *Time and Again Prayers*, compiled by Janet Cookson and Margaret Rogers; 12(b), 32(a), 41(a), 48(a), 58(a), from *Prayers and Hymns for Junior Schools*

Pitman Publishing: 45(a), from *Starting the Day*, J.T. Hilton

The Saint Andrew Press: 47(c) from *Sunday, Monday . . .*, R.S. Macnicol

Scholastic Publications: 78(d), which first appeared in *Child Education* magazine

SPCK: 37(c), 76(a), 78(a), 81(b), 85(a) from *A Brownie Guide to Prayer*, compiled by Rosalie Wakefield; 84(b), from *Baby's First Prayers*, A.C. Osborn Hann

Zinnia Symonds: 9(b), 20(a), 30(a), 38(c), 66(c), 75(d), 83(b), from *Let's Talk to God*; 35(b), 40(a), 42(a), 55(b), 56(d), 77(b), from *Let's Talk to God Again*, both published by Scripture Union

Schofield & Sims: 27(e)

Scripture Union: 13(a), 18(b) from *Family Prayers* (1971); 66(a) from *Family Prayers* (1974)

H.E. Walter Ltd: 28(c) from *Little Prayers for Little People*, Kathleen Partridge

Henry Z. Walck Inc: 68(a), from *First Prayers*